Gastric Band Hypnosis For Extreme Weight Loss: Hypnosis, Guided Meditations & Positive Affirmations For Rapid Fat Burn, Healthy Habits, Self-Love, Deep Sleep & Emotional Eating

By Visualiznation

Table of Contents

To the Narrator Total length of scripts is 5 hours 😊

Introduction
Mindfulness Body Scan
Letting go of our Past
Develop self-love Hour & half +

Diving Deep into Your Subconscious
End Emotional Eating
Overcoming Your Junk Food Cravings
Eating Smaller Portions Hour +

The Hypnotic Gastric Band
Self-Hypnosis For Weight Loss
Reinforcement Of Your Gastric Band
Deep Affirmations Hour & half +

Ego Strengthening For You
Power of Positive Self-Image
Waking Up 40 Minutes +
Emphasise a word or sentence

"..." means take a pause or breath while speaking before you continue.

Introduction

Thank you for choosing Gastric Band Hypnosis audio...and now thank yourself...for taking that *leap* forwards, towards a better version of you.

Every great move forward in your life begins with a *leap* of faith, a step into the unknown. The unknown can be scary and uncomfortable, but the rewards of being courageous far outweigh lingering in denial...and that is something that you are going to experience first hand...you have already taken your first step.

Hypnotic gastric band, also referred to as the *virtual* gastric band... will enable your Amygdala and Hippocampus, in the neocortex located inside of your brain...to believe that your stomach has shrunk to the size of a tennis ball. This will allow entry for only smaller amounts of food as we make you eat accordingly.

This meditation is split into four parts. The first section will cover the credentials you need...that will eventually allow you to install the virtual gastric band. In the second section you will be dissecting the issues holding you back head on...What are the problems?...Why they potentially aren't your fault?... And how we are going to replace them...with better things to worry about. The third section will be the installment of the virtual gastric band. The fourth and final section...designing a whole new you.

It is important to respect yourself, regardless of the decisions that you have made.. But it is just as important to recognise why you are...right here....right now... you are here.. to gradually achieve your dreams... Lose the weight that wants to be lossed... have a summer body all year round...and have a flexible, healthier lifestyle.

Here comes a reality check. Time! Time is a word that makes the quitters quit. You have suffered with your insecurity holding one leg down for so long now... but journeys, especially the most rewarding ones take...time. This is a journey... a weight loss journey....and what I mean by this is that there is a beginning and ending. The beginning will be tough, as your body is a survival machine and therefore does not like change, good or bad. It's too stupid to know that the change you are giving it...is going to make it *feel*... and *run*...*ten* times better. The ending is going to be glorious, and each and every day I want you to take a slither of the glory...and keep it in your pocket as a reminder of what is yet to come.

By taking that *leap* forward and listening to this audio, means that you have agreed to reinvent your belief system. And by listening to this audio on a daily basis...you will reinforce this amalgamation of new thoughts...creating a newer...and fitter you.

On that note...congratulations! As we now begin to start...that insecurity holding your one leg down...is already starting to lose its grip.

Mindfulness Body Scan

When you are ready...try to find a place....where your mind will be free from outside distractions.

Headphones may be useful and more effective....so that you can focus solely on the sound of my voice.

I would like you now...to find a comfortable position...either lying, or sitting...whatever is best for you in this moment.

Begin listening to this audio, only when you have arrived at your comfort.

The first meditation that we are going to perform...is just going to allow us to...tune in...and make sure...that we are nice and loose...and that any tension still left in your body...is ready to be relieved.

So without further ado, how about we begin.

When you are ready...I want you to let your eyes...peacefully...come to a close.
Now you are going to listen to the sound of my voice. Don't pay too much attention to the specific words said...instead.. notice the tone...the feel. Let the words just... float in &

out of your ears. In...and out....in...and out.

I want you to allow everything in your life at this moment...to be put on hold...as you take this time...for yourself.

You get so caught up in the stress that life throws your way... that you sometimes forget to tune in...and give yourself a little break...from your hardships.

Your attention...is now drifting it's focus on to the sound of my voice... and the sound of my voice...alone. As you continue to listen to each word I say, you allow yourself to relax... more...and more...and more.

You are going to start off....with a full scan of the body.

Our aim here is to make sure that each part

of your body is nice & relaxed...and at ease.

Each word I say... you allow yourself to

relax... more...and more...and more.

As we work our way through, I want you to imagine a beam of white light expanding on each body part you choose to focus on.

This beam of white light...will release the brain's control of your body...and relieve the tension inside your muscles. It will also allow yourself to relax...more...and more...and more.

Why don't we begin... by working our way up from the bottom of your feet...to the top of your head.

Ready?

A small white light begins to appear on the souls of both feet.

As this white light gradually expands... becoming larger and larger...the more your feet become more... and more...comfortable.

This white light is covering everything inside of your feet...and making sure it doesn't miss a single spot.

Massaging all the tissue and the muscles from within...this white light will take care of all the knots...pain...you are currently having...and soothe them all for you.

Now take a moment, and relax in this comfort. With your feet... now being nice and cozy... this white light slowly moves up...transitioning into your legs.

The transition feels nice...it gives you a tingling

sensation.

Don't try and move...just let this white light...take care of you.

The white light covers everything inside of your legs within its reach...as it did with your feet... giving them the exact same comfort.

Let it massage the tissue and the muscles.

As comfortable as July's air...you go to move your legs, but are unable to! As the white light has given them complete relaxation... and they now do not wish to be moved or used....for any physical strenuous activity...they are in total relaxation.

By yourself now, I want to give you the next five minutes, and let you have the opportunity to direct this, beaming white light through the upper half of your body.

I suggest you start with your stomach...then your chest...then your arms...followed by your neck...and then finally...let this white light...settle in your head.

Let your imagination commence when you are ready...

(Give them a five minute break)

(Also give a one minute warning with one minute

to go message...)

One more minute...let this white

light flow through...and relax the

entire body. **(One Minute)**

And with this white light finishing its job of relaxing your body...let it begin to fade peacefully while you rest.

Know that this white light can be easily accessed, and is on demand for you whenever you so need it, anytime of the day. Just come back here...and let the white light do its magic all over again.

Each word I say...you allow yourself to relax... more, and more. You are now going to practise a breathing exercise.

When I say so, I want you to take in a nice deep breath...hold it for a count of five...let your mind detach from everything it is currently attached to.. and then let it go.
Here, we begin.

Take a nice deep breath- in...count along with me....one…two…three…four…five...and…exhale, one...two...three...four...five...deep breath-breathe in…one… two…three…four…five ...exhale one...two..three...four...five...Again, breathe in…one… two…three…four…five...and ...exhale, one...two...three...four...five...deep breath in ….one… two...three…four…five...and ......exhale, one...two...three...four...five...One more... take a deep breath in...one, that's it...two...three...four...five...and...each word I say, you allow yourself to become... more....and more... relaxed.

Let's now allow your body to retake control of it's normal breathing pattern.

Amazing isn't it? Your body. Always there to support you in the millions of jobs it does for you every single second of the day. It's truly fascinating, a miracle of sorts.

Let's take a moment now to be mindful and appreciative of our bodies.

We all often neglect and forget, to be grateful to our bodies, to show them love...and care... but all that stops with you, right now. You are going to build a positive relationship with your body....from the inside... so that we can change it ...on the outside.

In between breaths, I want you to repeat

after me...silently or aloud...either way is

fine. **(Give them time to repeat)**

Breathe in...I admire....all the ways....my body takes care of me....and breathe out Breathe in...I want...to return the favour...and take care of my body...breeeathe out Breathe in with a big smile...my smile....is a way of showing... my body...love...and breathe out Breathe in...I admire....all the ways....my body takes care of me....and breathe out Breathe in...I want...to return the favour...and take care....of my body...breeeathe out Breathe in with a big smile...my smile....is a way of showing... my body...love...and breathe out

Last one, breathe in...me and my body...are going to work together...to build...our dreams...breathe out...and rest.

Scientific research has shown that positively talking to and about our bodies can have such a positive impact on our bodies health. I know, wow! I guess gratitude does reciprocate, what an incredible gift nature has given to us. Communication really is like casting a spell, and from here onwards...you are going to communicate better with your body.

No more running it down to yourself, no more running it down to your family and friends...and no more running it down...period!

It is an organic machine of love...and you are going to give it some.

Letting Go of Your Past

One of the very first things that we are going to acknowledge...is that the past is the past, and anything from the past that wants to enter the future with you... has to have permission, from only you, to do so.

Staying nice, and relaxed...just let your attention come back to my voice, and my voice alone.

In this journey, you are going to be climbing up a hill to get to your desired destination...and in order to reach the peak of this hill...you need to drop things that are pulling you down...we need...to let go of our past.

In this mediation you are going to develop a unique way of looking at the past. Perception is everything in life, and your perception is what needs to change. For it to change, there are a few things you must understand about how the past operates in the hippocampus, that is located inside of your brain.

The hippocampus... is where episodic memories are formed and indexed for later access. The hippocampus will often collect memories where your emotions are sky high. For example, If you were really really upset, or if you were really really happy... because the emotions were so

elevated...your brain attaches itself to them. Think back on a memory that you have, any memory.
I guarantee your emotions were high in that memory compared to your everyday emotions. You also often attach yourself to times when you have felt an emotion you had not until that moment felt before...for instance, your first heartbreak...or your first kiss.

Now that you understand how memories work...we must take a look at how science...sees the past.

The past is a tricky concept...and no one really knows for definite how it works...but we can point out the obvious and use it to our advantage.

I want you to imagine you are walking with a friend and you both see a car crash.
You may see it from one angle...and therefore blame it on the driver that you thought was in the wrong. However...your friend may have seen it from a different angle...and so blames it on the opposite driver.

When you go to sleep that night... you are convinced the past happened how you think the past happened.

Your friend on the other hand, is convinced that

the past happened how they saw it happen. Is

your past any less correct from theirs?

Let's say a few days later, you change your mind about what really happened and who was to blame...you now agree with your friend's version of what happened....but your opinion of the past could easily change back to how you saw it before...so... your brain's perception of the past is constantly shifting...according to how you think it really happened.

Does this mean that the past never really happened at all? No...the past happened for you to get where you are now...but it does mean...that we can control the way the past is recorded inside of our brain....through perception.

I know...that was a lot to take in so were are going to again bring our mind back to relaxation with a few deep breaths.

Nice and calm...count along with me... deep breath in...one... two...three...four...five...and...exhale,one...two...three...four...five...and deep breath in...one... two...three...four...five...and ...exhale, one...two...three...four...five...Gooood, breathe in...one... two...three...four...five...and ...exhale, one...two...three...four...five...and deep breath breathe in ....one... two...three...four...and ...exhale all the way out.

Stay here in this relaxation, and focus on your body's ability to take control of your normal breathing pattern.

Relaxed...I now want you to focus your awareness on the air, entering and leaving your nose What does it feel like on the edges of your nostrils?

What does it feel like when the breath is inside of your body?

How long are the gaps in between breaths?

Let that breath soothe, your brain and muscles

I want you for me now to…imagine the hairs all over your body
What do they feel like on your skin?

Do you have goosebumps?...or are your hairs just relaxing?

Now take a deep breath in...hold it for a count of five....four ...three…two...one, and exhale, one...two...three...four...five**...**count along with me...breathe in…one…
two…three…four…five...exhale,
one...two...three...four...five...breath
e in…one… two…three…four…and

...exhale all the way out...and relax.

I now want you to place

your attention...on the

space in between your ea I

want you to place a cloud

there.

A wet cloud...with lots...and lots of rain drops coming out of it.

Inside this cloud, is all of your memories floating around.

I want you to take one that brings you happiness. Take one that brings a warm feeling to your heart.

Think about...how this memory makes you feel?...How it made you felt?...When was it?...and most importantly...how it may have a positive effect on your life today? Take five minutes to answer all of these questions.

(Give them a five minute break)

Now I want you to do yourself a

favour...and put this memory into a

picture frame. Create an image on it,

that summarizes that memory.

I now want you to place it on top of your cloud...nice and safe.
I now want you to repeat this process... with another memory...another memory that brings you happiness. Again take five minutes to answer these questions so you can fully submerge yourself into this memory.

How does this memory make you feel?...How it made you felt?...When was it?...and how it may have a positive effect on your life today?

(Give them a five minute break)

Fantastic...now again put this memory into a picture frame...create a cover that summarises that beautiful memory...and place it on top of the cloud.

This cloud has no limit, no boundary...to how many memories of yours it can carry.
Count along with me...Breathe in…one…
two…three…four…five...exhale,one...two...three...f our...five...breathe
in...one...two...three...four...five….exhale,
one...two...three...four...five...last one, breathe in, one two….three...four..five..aaand exhaaale.

Inside the cloud...I want you to now bring your focus on to a bad memory that shouldn't and has no place inside there.

All it does is attract lightning for you...and you don't need a storm any longer.

With this bad memory in front of you... I want you to place it into a picture frame like you did with the happy ones.

Take that picture...and place it on the floor of the cloud.

I want you to watch that picture as

it disintegrates into water on the

cloud floor. You straight away feel

a sudden sense of relief.

That picture turns into water and that water exits the cloud through the clouds ongoing rain. Watch the picture disintegrate.

I now want you to focus on...how you feel...as the drops of water leave your cloud. leaving you.

For the next ten minutes...feel free to take all the distinct negative memories that you no longer want floating around with you...and let them go through your clouds rain. These negative memories might be ones that made you feel insecure about your weight...you feel held you back from doing something about your weight...or even bad memories that just don't want any longer because they are causing you distress.

Remember to acknowledge how it makes you feel when you let go of them...as this will change your brain's perception of that memory...and notify it, that it is no longer needed.

(Give them a ten minute break

(Also give them this two minute warning)...

Two minutes...get all those negative memories that have no further use for you...washed away out of your cloud.

(Two minutes)

Great! You did great! Feel the relief from letting go of those toxic memories.
You can always come back here at a later time to let more go.

This cloud is with you forever...and is under your control...and yours only.

Count along with me... breathe in…one… two…three…four…five...exhale,one...tw o...three...four...five...breathe in…one… two…three…four…five...and exhale, one...two...three...four...five...breathe in…one… two…three…four…five...and exhale all the way out, and...relax

Allow yourself now just to...move your shoulders gently...notice how...you, you feel a bit more freer than before...like a weight has been carried off off your shoulders.

Know that with...plenty of relaxation and...creative imagination...again, you can always come back here...to this space in between your ears... you can change your perception of a memory, by changing the way you look at it...or if you don't want it at all...you can just...let it wash away through your clouds rain.

Congratulations! You are making so much progress and are steps closer to being ready to install the virtual gastric band. You are on your way...to a new and improved you.

Develop Self Love

The next thing you will focus on...is...Developing Self Love.

Self Love, can mean a many deal of things...like talking to, and about yourself, with respect. Prioritising... and trusting yourself. Allowing yourself a break...from self-inflicted judgment. And forgiving yourself...when you may have been too harsh.

Despite that...one of the most important forms of Self Love...often overlooked, because honestly, honesty can be tough. That's right! Honesty.

Telling the truth to yourself is often avoided when it comes to hypnotherapy, as we like to hide from it, and then just hope it doesn't come back to bite us later.

You are here to lose weight, and keep that weight lossed...You are not here to lose weight, and then pile it all back on later. Like how so many success stories in the end play out.

Therefore, first of all we must realise...and come

to peace...with our previous mistakes...so that we can swap them with new and more efficient ones. As I continue to speak...I want you to find yourself becoming more and more relaxed....with each word I say.

Becoming more and more relaxed...with each word I say.

Relaxed...with each word I say. Know that this is going to be helpful, on your journey to losing weight...as we must highlight the issues beforehand...otherwise we end up with a brain, that has one set of beliefs on one side... and a different set on the other side.

Because giving up is easier, than trying your best...relaxed, with each word I say... we often fall victim to the set of beliefs that will bring us back to square one.

Honesty...Being honest to yourself...means being resilient to the truth...and being relaxed...with each word I say.

With that in awareness...right now, you are going to repeat after me.

(Give them plenty of time to repeat '...')

I am resilient ... and I am honest ... I have courage... and I am honest...I am resilient ... and I am honest ...I know myself ... and I am honest...I am resilient ... and I am honest ...I know my worth ... and I am honest...I am resilient ... I am honest...I don't lie ...especially not to myself...I am resilient ... and I am honest. Well done. Relax.

You are honest...and you are helping put a permanent smile on the face of the future you.

Now we are going to do a technique called mirroring. Mirroring is a fantastic method of changing our belief and behaviour system from within.

In order to get us relaxed, we are going to take in a few deep breaths.

So, here we go...count along with me breathe in...one... two...three...four...five...exhale, one...two...three...four...five...Breathe in...one... two...three...four...five...exhale, one...two...three...four...five...Breathe in...one... two...three...four...five...and exhale all the way out

Breathe in...one... two...three...four...five...exhale, one...two...three...four...five...Breathe in...one... two...three...four...five...exhale, one...two...three...four...five...Breathe in...one... two...three...four...five...and....exhaaale. Great

As you let your body return to its

normal breathing pattern...I wonder if you could imagine...being in your dream body...while sitting around a tab

Opposite you on this table, sits an unhealthy past model of you.
This model represents everything you dislike about yourself.

I want you now to...gather all the things you wish to change about yourself...and assign them to this old, model of you.

Be honest...be true to yourself...Honesty is Self Love.

(Give them a one minute break)

Relax and count along with me, breathe in…one… two…three…four…five...exhale, one...two...three...four...five...Breathe in…one… two…three…four…five...exhale, one...two...three...four...five...Breathe in…one…
two…three…four…five...and….breathe out

This old model of you...starts shoving all the food on the table into its mouth...it is a gruesome sight.
It makes you feel sick to watch.

I want you now to focus on what you look like,

in your dream body...and what they look like.

Focus on what you look like...in your dream

body...and what they, look like.

You are aware that the food on the table is available for you to take anytime you'd like, but!...while looking at this past model of you...I want you to repeat after me

(Give them plenty of time to repeat '...')

The truth can hurt... but I am honest ... I have courage... and I am honest... the truth can hurt...but I am honest ...I know myself ... and I am honest...the truth can hurt ... but I am honest ...I know my real worth ... and I am honest...the truth can hurt... but I am honest...I don't lie ...especially not to myself...I am resilient! ... and I, am honest. Good, relax.

The first step to healing... is coming to terms with the problem....and you...you are face to face with the problem... but instead of giving in, you have shown resilience! While looking at this past model of you for one last time, one last time...I want you to repeat after me.

(Give them plenty of time to repeat '...')

Even though...I made mistakes...I send my love... to the person opposite me...even though...I made mistakes...I send my love...to the person opposite me.

They were dealing with a lot...I send my love...to the person opposite me**...**they were dealing with a lot...but I send my love...to the person opposite me
Even though...I made mistakes...I send my love... to the person opposite me...they were dealing with a lot....but I send, my love...to that person opposite me

Send that person opposite you your love...and understand this...that the person you are now...in your dream body...is waiting for you.

When you are ready...slowly open up your eyes... and stay in your comfortable, relaxed position.

Well Done. You did brilliant! It can be hard to face our fears...but we have options and we always do...Forget everything and run...or face everything and rise... and oh my, you are rising.

Take this time to relax and feel good... as you have met your fears head on, and risen above them. Celebrate this accomplishment with your body, and smile.

Diving Deep into our Behaviours and Beliefs

You have learnt how to deal with your past and how to develop self love...but now...in this second section...you are going to focus on where the real change is going to take place...before we can finally install that virtual gastric band.

In this meditation...you are going to be diving deep into your behaviours and beliefs.

If we want to change...we must really take a detailed look as into why we are built the way we are built...and how to start again.

You may learn some things today, in this hour...that you never knew before...and some of it will blow your mind.

A word of warning...I am going to need you to put your thinking cap on as we practise self evaluation.

You see...yes, you are going to be diving deep into your behaviour and belief system...but really...you are going to be diving deep into your subconscious mind.

You may have already heard some of the wonders of the subconscious mind... or you may be a complete beginner ready to learn.

Inorder to get the full benefit and efficiency from this meditation...we are going to need to dissect and take a look at your previous system.

Find a comfortable position...seated or lying down...eyes open or eyes closed...whichever is best for you to concentrate. We suggest having your eyes closed for more effective learning and concentration.

Neuroscientists say that between birth and the age of seven... our subconscious mind operates at around 95 to 99%.

Your subconscious mind is like a sponge...and for you to survive it absorbs everything around you at an incredible rate.

I want you to think back to when you were a child...this was when your subconscious was even more prevalent in everyday activity. Take in for a second how amazing you were at picking up things so quickly...for example...your language.

Apart from an exceptional few... most people today, struggle to learn a new language besides the one that they already speak. But when you were a child you were picking up words and sentences at the speed of light.

The product of what you are today...derives from your early subconscious absorption. For example...people who are scared of dogs often had a bad experience with dogs when they were younger...and so this is how the subconscious operates that experience.

The dog barks at the child...the child feels fear and records that experience as frightening. Therefore, when the child next sees a dog...his or hers initial reaction, is to feel fear and be frightened.

Another example would be...a child sees people eating unhealthily and laughing...so the child assigns happiness to unhealthy eating. So now every time this person feels down they resort to eating rubbish, as they assume it will make them happy.

Throughout your life...you will have been told positive and negative things, that have shaped who you are as a person today. This is a result of your subconscious believing what was said. Your subconscious has no sense of humour and does not play jokes...it will believe anything you tell it, and anything others tell it.

You can't dodge toxic people...they are all around you and will always be. On the other hand, you can change, your subconscious beliefs. Changing your subconscious beliefs, will change your subconscious behaviours...and changing your subconscious behaviours, will change your life.

You might be thinking..."I must have so many unconscious programs that are the reason why I suffer with my weight and other things, how do I change my subconscious beliefs?"

Well...through repetition.

Whatever you put inside of your subconscious mind, and nourish it repeatedly...will eventually...become your reality.

In this practise of affirmations... we are going to be addressing a number of different topics and issues that may be deeply rooted in your subconscious, that may be causing you great harm. For instance...emotional eating.....junk food cravings...eating portions...and so on and so on.

Comfortable? Eyes Closed? Right...lets begin.

As we take in deep breaths...I want you to focus on the flow of the breath. The way it feels in your chest...the way it feels going through your nose...the temperature of the breath...is it refreshingly cold? Is it soothingly warm?

Count along with me,...breathe in...one...
two...three...four...five...exhale,
one...two...three...four...five...Breathe
in...one...
two...three...four...five...exhale,

one...two...three...four...five...Breathe in...one... two...three...four...five...and....exhale, relax........breathe in...one... two...three...four...five...exhale, one...two...three...four...five...Breathe in...one... two...three...four...five...exhale, one...two...three...four...five...Breathe in...one... two...three...four...five...and....breathe out.

Now that you are very relaxed...we are going to practise some affirmations.

Affirmations are a great way of communicating with your subconscious. When you are ready...repeat after me.

(Give them time to repeat '...')

Losing weight is easy for me.....I enjoy losing weight everyday....I show love and care for my body....I know I can easily achieve my goal...Count alone with me breathe in...one... two...three...four...five...exhale, one...two...three...four...five...Repeat after me, Losing weight is easy for me...because I can control how much I eat...I actually find it too easy to lose weight...it's a skill I was born with...breathe in...one... two...three...four...five...exhale, one...two...three...four...five...Losing weight is easy for me...I deserve to be slim...because I eat well everyday...so I will be thin...breathe in...one...

two…three…four…five...exhale, one...two...three...four...five…Losing weight is super easy for me...It's actually kind of fun...junk food makes me feel sick...so I won't do it again...breathe in…one… two…three…four…five...exhale, one...two...three...four...five...Last one, losing weight is easy for me...I just naturally lose weight...I'll have this skill forever...I am so lucky I lose weight easily...Breathe in…one… two…three…four…five...exhale, one...two...three...four...five…

Relax your feet...relax your legs...relax your arms and head...relax your chest .. and let the breath flow in and out...in....and out….in...and out...good

Now, we must show yourself some self-love as we face your fears.
In the next affirmation practise… we are going to revisit your fears...acknowledge them...and then change the way that we perceive them. Do you see how the skills you have learnt in the previous two chapters... are starting to come together? ..You are going to keep on using what you learn here to your advantage.

By changing the angle we look at them we

will be swapping these beliefs with new

ones. When you are ready...repeat after

me.

(Give them time to repeat '...')

Losing weight is easy for me...but it hasn't always been...I have learnt from my past...what's been, has been...breathe in...one... two...three...four...five...exhale, one...two...three...four...five...I have chosen to change my life....the past is far behind me....clearer now I see...losing weight is easier for me...breathe in...one... two...three...four...five...exhale, one...two...three...four...five...I have often neglected my health...but now I show my body love...it hasn't always been this way...but now, losing weight is easy for me...breathe in...one... two...three...four...five...exhale, one...two...three...four...five...I was damaging my body before...but now my body thanks me....losing weight is easy for me...losing weight is easy for me...breathe in...one... two...three...four...five...exhale, one...two...three...four...five...relax your body, relax your breath, relax your mind.

By you talking as if your goal has already been achieved...you bend the brain's perception of time and draw that dream closer and closer.

You are now going to do an exercise we called brick wall affirmations.

Brick wall affirmations is about you repeatedly throwing a sentence at a wall until the wall breaks.

I want you now to imagine a brick wall. Every brick on this wall...represents old habits.

We are going to break this wall with our words and engrain these messages straight to our subconscious.

Overcoming Your Junk Food Cravings

To combat your deeply rooted habits, you are now going to do an exercise we call brick wall affirmations.

Brick wall affirmations is about you repeatedly throwing a sentence at a virtual wall until the wall crashes down.
Junk food is an interesting concept. Most junk food is high in salt, sugars and fat...and so it triggers pleasure centers in our brains making us want to keep reaching, for more and more. No pleasure is temporary though...and so when the pleasure is over...we curl up in a ball...and feel terrible in our little sad corner.

This process will happen over and over and over until we decide to go on a stupid diet for one month...ignoring the fact that we deep down having actually addressed our harmful behaviours... and then guess what...the junk food cycle starts all back over again.

You normally eat junk food, because you convince yourself that you need to allow yourself to...““have a treat now and then””...when really a treat for your body is... good food... that helps it operate better.

Your body doesn't see bad food as a treat...your ego sees bad food as a treat...because your ego wants to feel the pleasure endorphins. Your body wants you to stop believing your ego and trusting your logic.

So, I want you now...to imagine a brick wall. Every brick on this wall...represents old habits.

You are going to break this wall with your words and engrain these messages straight to your subconscious.

Graffiti the word...Junk food...on the wall

Everytime you repeat an affirmation...this wall has a crack in the middle getting bigger and bigger

Now repeat after me

(Give them time to repeat '...')

Junk food makes me vomit...it makes me sick in my stomach...
Junk food makes me vomit...it makes me sick in my stomach...
Junk food makes me vomit...it makes me sick in my stomach....
Junk food makes me vomit...it makes me sick in my stomach....
Junk food does nothing for me...it sets me back to the beginning

Junk food does nothing for me...it sets me back to the beginning

Junk food does nothing for me...it sets me back to the beginning

Junk food does nothing for me...it sets me back to the beginning

I don't want to go back to the beginning...so I wouldn't even touch junk food I never want to go back to the beginning...so I wouldn't even touch junk food I don't want to go back to the beginning...so I won't listen to my stupid ego I don't want to go back to the beginning...so I won't listen to my stupid ego If I ever touched Junk food...I would be sick in my stomach

If I ever touched Junk food...I will think about eating junk

If I ever touched Junk food...I will think about eating junk

If I ever touched Junk food...I would be sick in my stomach

Junk food makes me vomit...it makes me sick in my stomach...

Junk food does nothing for me...it sets me back to the beginning

I don't want to go back to the beginning...so I wouldn't even touch junk food I don't want to go back to the beginning...so I won't listen to my stupid ego If I ever touched Junk food...I

would be sick in my stomach
If I ever touched Junk food...I will think about eating junk
Junk food makes me vomit...it makes me sick in my stomach...

Now let the wall smash and crumble into pieces.

Feels good! Feels like a weight has crumbled off of your shoulders.

End Emotional Eating

I now want you to make a new wall.

Emotional eating is an escape from your real problems. It is a way that your ego lets you forget what is really going on... and let's you have a quick few minutes of feel-good endorphins...again, pleasure is temporary...you curl up in a ball...and then feel terrible. Well not now! Not ever! You will repeat these affirmations on a daily basis and so next time you feel like eating junk...yucky mucky junk...you won't be eating it because you are bored...or stressed...or lonely...you will not allow it to enter you, at all!

I want you to graffiti on this wall...emotional, eating

Everytime you repeat an affirmation...this wall has a crack in the middle...getting bigger and bigger.

Now repeat after me

(Give them time to repeat '...')

Emotional eating is stupid...it preys on me when I am weak
Emotional eating is stupid...it preys on me when I am weak

Emotional eating is stupid...it preys on me when I am weak

Emotional eating is stupid...it preys on me when I am weak

I am not going to be weak when it comes to food... because I know, what's to be true I am not going to be weak when it comes to food... because I know, what's healthy I am not going to be weak when it comes to food... because I know, what's to be true I am not going to be weak when it comes to food... because I know, what's healthy

Being upset actually makes me want to eat more healthy...Bad food, equals a bad mood Being upset actually makes me want to eat more healthy...Bad food, equals a bad mood Being upset makes me want to eat more healthy...Bad food, makes a bad mood Being upset makes me want to eat more healthy...Make bad food, make a bad mood I am true to myself...even when I am down

I am true to myself...even when I am down

I am true to myself...even when I am down

No matter whether I am up or down...I stay true to myself

Emotional eating is stupid...it preys on me when I am weak

I am not going to be weak when it comes to food... because I know, what's to be true I am not going to be weak when it comes to food... because I know, what's healthy

Being upset actually makes me want to eat more healthy...Bad food, equals a bad mood Being upset makes me want to eat more healthy...Make bad food, make a bad mood I am true to myself...even when I am down
No matter whether I am up or down...I stay true to myself

Let that wall fall… and let your shoulders...relax.

Eating Smaller Portions

Nutritionists say...that even trimming your portions down by 10% to 20%...regardless of body type...endomorph, mesomorph or ectomorph...you will cut a considerable amount of weight if it is kept up constantly.

I want you now to make your final wall.

Graffiti on it...Big meals.

Everytime you repeat an affirmation...this wall has a crack in the middle...getting bigger and bigger.

Now repeat after me

(Give them time to repeat '...')

I know what is right...and I know what is wrong
I know what is right...and I know what is wrong
I know what is right...and I know what is wrong
I know what is right...and I know what is wrong
There is a balance...and I will not cross my line
There is a balance...and I will not cross my line
There is a balance...and I will not cross my line
There is a balance...and I will not cross my line
I know what is right and wrong...and I will not cross my line

I know what is right and wrong...and I will not cross my line

Losing weight is easy for me.....I enjoy losing weight everyday....I show love and care for my body....I know I can easily achieve my goal...

Losing weight is easy for me...because I can control how much I eat...I actually find it too easy to lose weight...it's a skill I was born with...

Losing weight is easy for me...I deserve to be slim...because I eat well everyday...so I will be thin...

Losing weight is super easy for me...It's actually kind of fun...junk food makes me feel terrible...so I wont do it again...

Losing weight is easy for me...I just naturally lose weight...my gastric band is ready to come on...I have a friend who is going to take care of that for me...And relax

Great! Absolutely brilliant! By repeating all of those affirmations and by using the brick wall technique every other day...you will be reinforcing those new beliefs into your subconscious...and over time... your behaviours will change and a new you will emerge.

In the next section of this meditation we will be installing your virtual gastric band.

The Hypnotic Gastric Band

This is it...now that you have learned to face your fears and change your perception of the past...it is time that you install the virtual gastric band.

You are now going to enter the right side of your brain and play around with your frontal cortex. This part has many functions but one of its primary, is controlling creativity and imagination.

So, eyes closed and staying relaxed...you are going to challenge yourself. I want you to imagine the tip of your nose.

How about the nails of your toenails?

I wonder if you can imagine the bones in your hands?

What about the saliva on your tongue?

The veins all around your body?

Now...how about the darkness?...do you notice how everything, everywhere... is pure darkness when your eyes are shut? But you were just imagining things with colour and forgot all about the darkness. In science we call this...working from the matter to

change the field.
I want you to rest in this darkness...sink into it…focus on it….let it consume your sense of your surroundings.

As you drop deeper and deeper into this darkness you become more and more disconnected from earth...more and more disconnected from your body, and its location.

Relax...let go.

Behind your closed eyes... is relaxing darkness...sink deeper and deeper into the relaxing darkness behind your closed eyes.

Behind your closed eyes... is relaxing darkness...sink deeper and deeper into the relaxing darkness behind your closed eyes.

Behind your closed eyes...sink deeper and deeper into the relaxing darkness behind your closed eyes.

Ten...Darkness...Nine...Deeper...Eight...Relax...S even...Darkness...Six...Deeper...Five...Relax... Four…Darkness...Three...Deeper...Two…Relax... One...Darkness...Zero...Deeper And...Relax

Imagine you are standing in a black room...with no walls or boundaries...It is not cold, nor warm, it is just right.

You turn around and in front of you stands millions upon millions of versions of you…identical in the face and body.

Each of these millions of versions of yourself have an individual job they take care of inside of your body

They work for you and will do anything that you ask them to with one hundred percent perfection. You can come here and talk to them whenever you desire to.

I want you to call out and bring forward whoever is incharge of your gastric band.

In the distance you see the version of you who controls your gastric band making their way through the crowd.

As you wait for them to reach you…you start to feel excitement brewing inside of you...as this is the moment that you have been waiting for, for so long now. It's finally here!

Arriving by your side, you click your finger… and all of the other millions of you's that you don't need, for now, instantly vanish.
It is now just you and the version of you who controls your gastric band, standing either side of one another.

I want you to give this version of you controlling

your gastric band a name...take a second, think of a name you'd like to allocate it to.

Got one? Great!

This person belongs inside your subconscious...and therefore works inside of your body to suit your very wants and needs.

Ten...Darkness...Nine...Deeper...Eight...Relax

Because this person lives within your subconscious...you must communicate with them through repetitive affirmations.

Seven...Darkness...Six...Deeper...Five...Relax...

I want you to imagine...your subconscious friend who controls your gastric band...is in a doctors uniform.

Four...Darkness...Three...Deeper...Two...Relax...

They lay their hands, gently onto your eyes...and close them...Ten...Darkness...Nine...Deeper...Eight...Relax...Seven...Darkness...Six...Deeper...Five...Relax...Four...Darkness...Three...Deeper...Two...Relax...One...Darkness...Zero...Deeper And...Relax

(Give them time to repeat '...')

Repeat after me...What is my goal?...

I want to lose weight...I want to be healthy...
I want to lose weight...I want to be healthy...
I want to lose weight...I want to be healthy...
I want to lose weight...I want to be healthy...

I want to lose weight...I want to be healthy...
I want to lose weight...I want to be healthy...
I want to lose weight...I want to be healthy...
I want to lose weight...I want to be healthy...

Your gastric band is coming on your stomach is contracting...breathe
in...one...two...three...four...five...exhale...one...two ...three...four...five...darkness...deeper...relax
To really hit the message home...it would help if you imagine the words that you are passing on. It would become even more ingrained...if you also add emotion to these images.

(Give them time to repeat '...')

Repeat after me...what do I want to look like?...

I want to be thin...I want to look good...
I want to be thin...I want to look good..
I want to be thin...I want to look good...
I want to be thin...I want to look good...

I want to be thin...I want to look good...
I want to be thin...I want to look good...

I want to be thin...I want to look good...
I want to be thin...I want to look good...

Your gastric band is coming on, your stomach is contracting....it doesn't hurt...it feels natural..it feels like it wants the gastric band...breathe in...one...two...three...four...five...exhale...one...tw

o...three...four...five...darkness...deeper...relax

(Give them time to repeat '...')

Repeat after me..Why do I want to look like this?

I want to feel good...I want to feel confident...
I want to feel good...I want to feel confident...
I want to feel good...I want to feel confident...
I want to feel good...I want to feel confident...

I want to feel good...I want to feel confident...
I want to feel good...I want to feel confident...
I want to feel good...I want to feel confident...
I want to feel good...I want to feel confident...

Your gastric band is coming on, your stomach is contracting...breathe in...one...two...three...four...five...exhale...one...tw

o...three...four...five...darkness...deeper...relax

(Give them time to repeat '...')

Repeat after me..What will it do for my happiness?.

It will make me happy...it will put a smile on my face...
It will make me happy...it will put a smile on my face...
It will make me happy...it will put a smile on my face....
It will make me happy...it will put a smile on my face...

A tighter waist...a smile on my face...
A smile on my face...because of my tighter waist...
It will make me happy...it will put a smile on my face...
It will make me happy...it will put a smile on my face...

Your gastric band is coming on, your stomach is contracting...breathe
in...one...two...three...four...five...exhale...one...tw

o...three...four...five...darkness...deeper...relax

(Give them time to repeat '...')

Repeat after me...and how can a virtual gastric band help me achieve it?

It will shrink my stomach...it will stop mass consuming...
It will shrink my stomach...it will stop mass consuming...

It will shrink my stomach...it will stop mass consuming...
It will shrink my stomach...it will stop mass consuming...

It will shrink my stomach...it will stop mass consuming...
It will shrink my stomach...it will stop mass consuming...
It will shrink my stomach...it will stop mass consuming...
It will shrink my stomach...it will stop mass consuming...

Your gastric band...is on...food will now be processed slower...mass consuming will now stop...weight loss is now in implementation...breathe in...one...two...three...four...five...exhale...one...two...three...four...five...feel the weight already starting to slowly melt off.

Ten...Darkness...Nine...Deeper...Eight...Relax...Seven...Darkness...Six...Deeper...Five...Relax... Four...Darkness...Three...Deeper...Two...Relax... One...Darkness...Zero...Deeper And...Relax...

Inside this dark room...behind your closed eyes...your subconscious friend, in charge of your gastric band, opens your eyes.

Standing up, you look down...you realise you

are standing and existing in your dream body.

Go on! Move around...notice how it feels...physically...and emotionally.

(Give a two minute break)

Ten...Light...Nine...Rise...Eight...Relax...Seven...Li ght...Six...Rise...Five...Relax...Four...Light... Three...Rise...Two...Relax...One...Light...Zero...Ris e... and...Relax.

How great does it feel? To be in your dream body?

Ten...Light...Nine...Rise...Eight...Relax...now, still keeping them eyes closed and without imagining anything for a moment, reconnect to your physical body and recollect how that feeling felt...to be in your dream body.

Seven...Light...Six...Rise...Five...Relax...know that your subconscious friend controlling your gastric band is working all hours of the day, keeping that gastric band in place.

Four...Light...Three...Rise...Two...Relax...

Holding on to the feeling of achieving your dream body...this is how you can let your body...and your subconscious friend know...that you still want the gastric band on...by eating healthier...by taking

care and having respect for yourself, even when you are down...by knowing that you are on the right path, trusting your subconscious friend...and by thinking positive thoughts when
thinking about your gastric band.

All of this will reinforce your goals into your subconscious mind...and keep that gastric band wrapped tightly around your stomach.

Ten...Light...Nine...Rise...Eight...Relax...Seven... Light...Six...Rise...Five...Relax...Four...Light... Three...Rise...Two...Relax...One...Light...Zero...R ise... and...Relax.

In your own time...open your eyes and again pay attention to that feeling of glory. Yes! You can feel this way, even with your eyes open! And by doing so you are making that journey quicker and easier on yourself.

With the help from your creative mind anything is possible in the matter of the field. Well Done! You did fantastic!

Self-Hypnosis For Weight Loss

This upcoming meditations purpose is to reinforce the gastric band in your subconscious...and to assist you, in a Self-hypnosis weigh loss technique. This technique can be easily adopted and used for a later time as well as now.

When you are ready...find a place, where your mind will be free from outside distractions. This meditation can be done in the shower, or out, either way is fine.
Headphones may be useful if you are not in the shower so that you can focus solely on the sound of my voice. Please do not, wear headphones or carry any electrical device in the shower.

I would like you now... to find a comfortable stance or position...either standing, or lying...whatever is best for you in this moment.

To start...we are going to practise some breathing.

Count along with me...breathe in...one... two...three...four...five...exhale, one...two...three...four...five...breathe in...one... two...three...void...five...exhale, one...two...three...void...five...breathe in...one... two...three...four...five...and....exhale...relax.

Every number that you say...sends you deeper and deeper into relaxation...deeper and deeper into that dark void, closer and closer to your core...breathe in...one... two...three...four...five...exhale, one...two...three...four...five...breath e in...one... two...three...four...five...exhale, one...two...three...four...five...breath e in...one... two...three...four...five...and....bre athe out.

Every number you say...deeper and deeper you sink into that dark relaxing void...closer and closer to your core.

Breathe in...one... two...three...four...five...exhale, one...two...three...four...five...breathe in...one... two...three...four...five...exhale, one...two...three...four...five...last one, breathe in...one... two...three...four...five...and....breathe all the way out and...relax.

In the dark void...close to your core...I wonder if

you could, imagine the freckles on your back.

How about the hairs on top of your head?

I wonder if you can imagine

your cloud of memories... in

between your ears? What about

the space in between your

toes?

The blood all around your body?

Now I want you to refocus your awareness on your breath...as you relax deeper and deeper into that dark space, closer and closer to your core..

Sink into it...deeper and deeper...closer and closer...relax.

Breathe....let your breath flow peacefully.

I now want you to visualize yourself in your shower. Focus on your surroundings

The temperature of the room.

The smell of the room.

The temperature of the water?

The feeling of comfort as the water hits your skin.

More...and more...relaxed. Enjoy the coziness of this shower more...and more relaxed.

Inside the shower...I now want you to look down, and see the water shedding layers of fat off of your body.

It feels amazing...like weight is just melting off.

Reinforcement of Your Gastric Band

You are now going to take some deep breaths in this shower, while the water continues to melt layers of fat off of your body.

Count along with me...breathe in...one... two...three...four...five...exhale, one...two...three...four...five...breathe in...one... two...three...four...five...exhale, one...two...three...four...five...breathe in...one... two...three...four...five...and... exhale, relax...now stop counting...and instead enjoy the warm water...enjoy the fat melting off of you...enjoy this experience...breathe in...one... two...three...four...five...exhale, one...two...three...four...five...breathe in...**(Count of five)**...breath out...**(Count of five)**....breathe in..**(Count of five)**...breathe out...**(Count of five)**

In this warm....pleasant shower...I want you now to take time...and thank your subconscious friend...I want you now to take time...and thank your gastric band.

Let the feeling of gratitude run deep throughout your body.

Breathe in...**(Count of THREE)**...breath out...**(Count of three)**....breathe in..**(Count of three)**...breathe out...**(Count of three)** Let your relaxed body...return to its natural breathing pattern...as you grow, closer..and closer..to your core...underneath this warm shower. **Very Short Pause**

Let the water flush away your fears...flush away your problems...and flush away any excess tension out of your body.

Deep Affirmations

Under this cozy stream of warm water... you are now going to speak the deepest affirmations you have done....while staying relaxed, underneath this cozy stream of warm water...closer and closer to your core...more and more weight being lossed. Repeat after me.

(Give them time to repeat '...')

The warm skilky water...covering my body...is melting off my weight
The warm skilky water...covering my body...is melting off my weight
My gastric band is on...and I am enjoying...this warm water
My gastric band is on...and I am enjoying...this warm water
Everytime... I am in the shower...weight is falling off of my body
Everytime... I am in the shower...weight is falling off of my body
I can come here... and lose weight...anytime I want
I can come here... and lose weight...anytime I want
My subconscious friend...is working...to make me slimmer
My subconscious friend...is working...to make me thinner
I have changed my beliefs...I have changed my behaviours...I have changed my ways I have

changed my beliefs...I have changed my behaviours...I have changed my ways They are no longer my ways...they are no longer my beliefs...they are no longer my behaviors They are no longer my ways...they are no longer my beliefs...they are no longer my behaviors My gastric band...and my new belief system...are going to make me thin My gastric band...and my new set of beliefs...are going to make me slim Losing weight is easy for me...because I do these meditations daily
I do these meditations daily...so losing weight is easy for me

Let the water flush away your fears...flush away your problems...and flush away any tension inside your body.

Repeat after me.

(Give them time to repeat '...')

Every time I am in the shower...every time I am sleeping...weight is falling off of me Every time I am sleeping...every time I am in the shower...weight is falling off of me I go to sleep early...and I do not stress...so weight drops off of me easily I go to sleep early...and I do not stress...so weight drops off of me easily Weight falls off of me easily...because my subconscious friend...has my back all day everyday Weight falls off of me easily...because my subconscious friend..all day everyday, has my back Even when

I am down...even when I no longer have faith...my subconscious friend has my gastric band on, because they care

Even when I no longer have faith...even when I am down...my subconscious friend has my gastric band on, because they care

Subconsciously I know...my past is my past...and I am a new, better and determined version of myself

My past is my past...but subconsciously I know...I am a new, better and determined version of myself

I am aware...that I am losing weight

I am aware...that I am losing weight

I am aware...that I am losing weight

I am proud...that I am losing weight...and relax

Let the shower slowly come an end.

Despite the water, no longer flowing...your body is still warm, and you are even more determined to drop even more weight.

Count along with me...breathe in...one... two...three...four...five...exhale, one...two...three...four...five...breathe in...one... two...three...four...five...exhale, one...two...three...four...five...breathe in...one... two...three...four...five...exhale all the way out and let your eyes gradually reopen.

Stay in whatever position that you are in for a

moment, and rest.

I want you to know that everytime you are sleeping...every time you are in the shower...every time you are making the right decisions...no matter what your ego is telling you...with your subconscious friend and gastric band supporting you...you are taking steps, closer and closer...towards your ideal body....you are doing brilliant as we enter the last and final section.

Ego Strengthening For You

In the final section of this meditation practise...we are going to be building your self-confidence and self-esteem through strengthening your ego.

Ego strengthening is essential when it comes to personal happiness and well-being. It is also very important so that you can make the right decisions and *stay*, on the right path.

Even with your brain tightening your body's stomach...you will still bump into many distractions that are going to try and throw you off route to losing weight. People with low ego-strength often find themselves being overwhelmed by reality...and so listening to this section daily will increase your ego-strength, and will help you make sure this never happens to you.
When you are ready...find a place where you will be free from outside interruption.

Now if you can find a comfortable position...either lying, or sitting...whatever is best for you right now in this moment.

For me now...close your eyes and rest.

(Three second gaps '...')

We are going to start with a breathing exercise...breathe in...hold...exhale...hold...breathe in...hold...exhale...hold....last one, breathe in...hold...exhale...and rest.

Do you ever find yourself in the mirror critiquing *every* little thing about yourself?...Some countries in the east but predominantly in the west...we have built a socially constructed habit, as to where everyone is in competition with everyone else...we have actually unlearned the ability to feel good by our own standards.

Like section one...this has a lot to do with, *perception*.

It is no secret that *today*, big social media companies and media in general have made us insecure and anxious about the way we look...where we are in this journey called *'got to get rich as soon as possible'* ...and this has had a huge impact on the way we treat ourselves and others.

In this meditation you are going to be practising a technique we call *identical visualisation*. Identical visualization is a great practise for being able to change unhealthy habits that are...making you feel worthless...promoting you to put on more weight...destroying your relationships.

I would like to now bring your attention to a quote that has the *power* to *change* lives...'How you do *anything*...is how you do *everything*'. What essentially this quote means is that...your attitude towards one thing, is often your attitude towards everything. Most people think that if you change the way you look at your weight you will have changed the way you look at your weight...but really...if you change the way you look at your weight, you will have changed the way you look at everything...work...family...friends...love...and so on. You see, weight loss isn't just about gastric bands, surgery, diet, and exercise...sure, all of those things make a huge difference... but if you don't change your attitude... your perception towards something...you won't have changed your attitude and perception towards anything... and that will just land you back at square one. Your gastric band needs you to cooperate with it.

On that note...if they weren't already, please close your eyes. Every word I say now...just find yourself drifting into relaxation with every word I say now. What you are going to do...identical visualization... is in basic terms...putting yourself in a real life everyday scenario, and behaving differently than usual.

No matter how dark this gets...remember that there is always a method behind the madness. I want you to first, *imagine* that you are around a dinner table with your family...or your friends, eating food.

Take time to picture everything and everyone

around you vividly and with great detail...the *clearer* the image, the *clearer* the message is to your subconscious.

Got all you need? Take a few

more seconds to really make

this image crisp. Brilliant. Let's

imagine a friend or family

member brings out a desert.

You know...that you have eaten healthy that

week...and so you are allowed to take a bite.

How good does this food smell?

How good does this food taste?

Go ahead, enjoy it!

Your friend or family member then serves you another plate.

You know that you should not have another slice as it would be setting yourself back...you pick up your fork and have another slice anyway.

After eating another slice...you can't help but feel

terrible...as if you know what your goal is, and that you are moving in the complete opposite direction...

Good, let your subconscious mind know that this behaviour is not right.

(Three second gaps '...')

Breathe
in...hold...exhale...hold...brea
the
in...hold...exhale...hold....bre
athe
in...hold...exhale...breathe
in...hold...exhale...hold...

Deep breath in...hold...exhale...hold....breathe in...hold...exhale...hold...last one, breathe in...hold...exhale...and relax. I now want you to imagine that you are standing in the middle of your kitchen.

Take time to picture everything around you vividly and with great detail...*remember*, the *clearer* the image, the *clearer* the message is to your subconscious mind.

Inside your kitchen...I want you to go to where you keep your treats.
I now want you to open the draw, the fridge,

the cupboard...wherever you keep your

treats. Inside, is your *favourite* treat. You

can't help but be *drawn* to pick it up and eat

it. Feeling an irresistible urge...you eat it.

Even one bite in...you yet again feel terrible for acting in the complete opposite way that would need to, to achieve your dream body.

(Three second gaps '...')

breathe
in...hold...exhale...hold...bre
athe
in...hold...exhale...hold....bre
athe
in...hold...exhale...breathe
in...hold...exhale...hold...

Deep breath
in...hold...exhale...hold....breathe
in...hold...exhale...hold...last one, breathe
in...hold...exhale...hold, and relax.

I want you to now visualize being in your bathroom, looking at yourself through your bathroom mirror.

Take time to picture your surroundings in great detail.

Looking at yourself through the bathroom

mirror...I want you now to take note of most of the things that you *negatively* take note of, about yourself.

I want you to understand that these perceptions...can be changed by counteractive actions.

Power of Positive Self-Image

On that note, I want you to return your thoughts back to the dinner table with your family...or your friends, eating the desert.

Let's now reimagine all of these events.

Your friend or family member brings out a desert.

You know...that you have eaten healthy that week, and so you are allowed to take a bite.
You enjoy it like you did before...but now it is that time where your friend or family brings you another slice of the desert.

You know from your previous mistake that you should not have another slice as it would be setting yourself back...you pick up your fork and go to place it into the desert anway *but*...stop midway.

I want you to stay here for a moment...in between deciding whether to jeopardise your success and have another bite...or be sensible, and put the fork down.

You really really deeply feel the urge to take another bite.

Right now...I want you to imagine what your *dishonorable ego* would be trying to tell you...versus what your *responsible body* is trying to tell you. Which one are you going to listen to?

Knowing that your body is correct...you put down your fork, *back* on to the table...and push the plate holding the desert away from you.

This feels good to you...like you know what your goal is and that you are moving in the right direction to achieve it.

(Three second gaps '...')

breathe
in...hold...exhale...hold...bre
athe
in...hold...exhale...hold....bre
athe
in...hold...exhale...breathe
in...hold...exhale...hold...

Deep breath in...hold...exhale...hold....breathe in...hold...exhale...hold...last one, breathe in...hold...exhale...and relax. I now want you to imagine that you are standing in the middle of your kitchen again.

Take time to picture everything around you vividly and with great detail...*remember*, the *clearer* the image, the *clearer* the message is to your subconscious mind.

Inside your kitchen...I want you to revisit where you keep your treats.

I now want you to open the draw, the fridge, the cupboard...wherever you keep your treats...and stare right back at it again.

I want you to stay here for a moment...rethink about what your *dishonorable ego* would be trying to tell you...versus what your *responsible body* is trying to tell you. Which one are you going to listen to?
Once again...knowing that your body is correct...you do what you have to do to separate yourself from this treat.

Feel a sense of accomplishment...feel proud about your actions to better yourself.

(Three second gaps '...')

Breathe
in...hold...exhale...hold...brea
the
in...hold...exhale...hold....bre
athe
in...hold...exhale...breathe
in...hold...exhale...hold...

Deep breath
in...hold...exhale...hold....breathe
in...hold...exhale...hold...last one, breathe
in...hold...exhale...hold, and relax.

I want you to now revisualize being in your bathroom, looking at yourself through your bathroom mirror.

Take time to picture your surroundings in great detail.

Looking at yourself through the bathroom mirror...I want you now to take note of the *positive* things to take note of about yourself.

This doesn't have to consist of just appearance...this can also be personality traits you admire yourself for having. Take time... be less harsh and more honest...really gather and collect all the good things about yourself.

(Give them a one minute break)

I now want you to take some of your best qualities and put them into a powerful affirmation.

If you could make five that would be great...if you could make *ten!* that would be amazing. Take some time and make a few...be creative.

(Give them a one minute break)

If you struggled making any...dont worry...just use ones like 'I am beautiful in every aspect' or... 'I am kind to others'. If you got around five to ten affirmations in place, brilliant! Now...without me... I want *you* to repeat *your* affirmations and mantras to yourself. You can do this! With five minutes...mix between them at free will and say whatever positive things float to your mind!

(Give them a five minute break)

And relax...

(Three second gaps '...')
Eyes remaining closed...behind those closed eyes...breathe in...hold...exhale...hold...breathe in...hold...exhale...hold....breathe in...hold...exhale...hold...breathe in...hold...exhale all the way out.

Waking Up

Well done you!

You have done an incredible job, throughout this whole thing. You have learnt how to develop self love and let go of your past...dive deep into your subconscious mind and confront issues holding you back...build a relationship with your subconscious mind through your subconscious friend....install your virtual gastric band through your subconscious friend...and then you have learnt most importantly how attitude towards one thing can change your attitude towards everything.

As we come to a close..I want to remind you that listening to each one of these four sections every other week or month isn't going to keep your stomach tight...your gastric band tight...or help you change your behaviours and beliefs.

Ideally, one of these four sections should be listened to everyday or on a regular basis for it to have an effect on your mental and physical health.

You should be really proud of yourself...this is only the start of a marvellous journey ahead for you...I know it!

Thank you for choosing Gastric Band Hypnosis audio...and now thank yourself, for taking that leap forwards...towards a better version of you.

Introduction
Mindfulness Body Scan
Letting go of Your Past
Developing Self Love
Diving Deep into Your Subconscious
Overcoming Your Junk Food Cravings
End Emotional Eating
Eating Smaller Portions
The Hypnotic Gastric Band
Self-Hypnosis For Weight Loss
Reinforcement Of Your Gastric Band
Deep Affirmations
Ego Strengthening For You
Power of Positive Self-Image
Waking Up

CPSIA information can be obtained
at www.ICGtesting.com
Printed in the USA
LVHW060102260521
688251LV00002BA/240

9 781801 345903